WHAT HAPPENED TO JUDAH?

BY

GLADYS TAYLOR

THE COVENANT PUBLISHING CO. LTD.
121, Low Etherley, Bishop Auckland, Co. Durham, DL14 0HA

2011

Revised and reprinted 2011

ISBN 978-085205-088-0

Printed by
THE COVENANT PUBLISHING COMPANY LIMITED
121, Low Etherley, Bishop Auckland,
Co. Durham, DL14 0HA
www.covpub.co.uk

Gladys Taylor was a prominent figure for many years in the Research Department of B.I.W.F. and delivered memorable lectures on our heritage and that of the Early Church in Britain.

WHAT HAPPENED TO JUDAH?

When one approaches British-Israel teaching for the first time, the question most likely to arise is, "if we are Israel, why are we so unlike the Jews?" A straightforward and brief answer to this obvious question would be, "Because most of the Jews are not really Israelites." Such a reply would be correct but hopelessly puzzling to most people, unless followed immediately by a detailed account of the respective histories of the separate and distinct kingdoms of Israel and Judah. The identity of the Jews is bound up with the history of the tribe of Judah, which is so complex in its divisions as to demand a separate study.

The Independent Tribe

The tribe of Judah appears to have shown its independence from the time of Jacob onward. Among the patriarch's sons, Judah seems to have been leader. The older sons had been dismissed from the birthright responsibility because of weaknesses that disqualified them: Reuben was morally unstable; Simeon and Levi had shown cruel traits of character. Judah, who was evidently of attractive appearance, assumed the position of leadership. He acted as spokesman for the sons of Jacob and he seems to have held the "sceptre," or rod of office, significant of leadership. There is good reason for believing that there was such a rod of office in the Hebrew family from the earliest times and its possession by Judah was confirmed in the divinely inspired promise given to his family by Jacob, "The sceptre shall not depart from Judah, nor a lawgiver from between his feet, until Shiloh come."[1] The promise is a long one and we will not deal with the many other details here, but it is evident that Judah was being

---

[1] *Genesis* 49:10

singled out for rulership, though the throne was not to be seen in Israel until many generations later.

Joseph's Leadership

There was another form of headship in Israel, of a very practical kind, which was given because of merit to Joseph, who was much younger than his brother Judah. This was confirmed in the separate blessings given by Jacob to the sons of Joseph, Ephraim and Manasseh, before his blessing of the respective tribes took place. One may define these two forms of leadership as the official office of ruler, given with the sceptre to Judah, and the practical administration of national matters given to Joseph. Just as the boy who was taken as a slave to Egypt was to rescue the land from famine in later years— even distributing food beyond Egypt's boundaries—so Israel was to fulfil a similar function in the world, in centuries to come. At the same time, the tribe of Judah was to provide the kingly House of David, to rule over the people of Israel in perpetuity and, as we find from our researches, to provide kings for other nations, too. Both these promises, to Joseph and Judah, were to have wider implications than appeared at the time they were given. As we may imagine, such a division of leadership was bound to result in some friction and jealousy—usually on the part of Judah—but these matters were the concern of Almighty God and the building of His future Kingdom. Petty jealousies were unimportant against the broad scope of His plan.

The Divided Nation

There were times when ambition and envy brought about clashes between Joseph and Judah. The characteristics seen in the sons of Jacob showed themselves later in the tribes descended from them.

When after the death of Solomon, the children of Israel divided into two kingdoms, the division seems to have come about instinctively. It only required a crisis in the nation's life to make the split complete. It is comforting to know that, when our own weaknesses bring about unfortunate circumstances, God, Who foresees all things, will use the very results of our folly to contribute to the purposes of His Kingdom. This is what happened when the twelve tribes divided into the two kingdoms of Israel and Judah. So much so, that God declared, "this thing is done of me," and sent a message to Rehoboam to halt his proposed campaign against the ten tribes by which he intended to bring them back under his rule.[2] Any great emperor may order the movements of nations under his domination but only Almighty God can foresee the actions of individuals and the characteristics of nations, so as to plan His campaign unerringly in advance of human decisions. The divisions within Israel were always used in fulfilment of His Kingdom plan from the earliest times. The family of Judah was itself divided a number of times, always with an important objective in view. The family inheritance passed to the twin sons of Judah, Pharez and Zarah. God had disinherited his first two sons, because of wickedness for which they were punished by death. They died childless.[3] Judah's third son, Shelah, who like his two elder brothers was the child of a Canaanitish woman, lived to become the father of a tribal group, but was also set aside in the matter of the family heritage as concerning the throne.

---

[2] II *Chronicles* 11
[3] *Genesis* 38:7

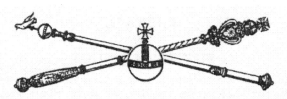

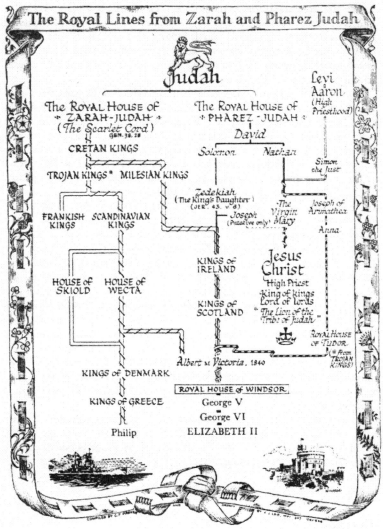

Judah

The Royal House of ZARAH-JUDAH
(The Scarlet Cord) GEN. 38.28

CRETAN KINGS

TROJAN KINGS*   MILESIAN KINGS

FRANKISH KINGS   SCANDINAVIAN KINGS

HOUSE of SKIOLD   HOUSE of WECTA

KINGS of DENMARK

KINGS of GREECE

Philip

The Royal House of PHAREZ-JUDAH

David

Solomon   Nathan

Zedekiah (The King's Daughter) (JER. 43. v 6)

Joseph (Putative only)

KINGS of IRELAND

KINGS of SCOTLAND

Albert м *Victoria*, 1840

ROYAL HOUSE of WINDSOR

George V
=
George VI
=
ELIZABETH II

Levi
Aaron
(High Priesthood)

Simon the Just

Joseph of Arimathea

Anna

The Virgin Mary

Jesus Christ
High Priest
King of kings
Lord of lords
"The Lion of the Tribe of Judah"

Royal House of Tudor
(* From TROJAN KINGS)

8

An Early Dispersion

God had made it plain, from the beginning, that He was selecting both the patriarchs *and* their wives. Israel knew the basic rules, long before they were codified into laws at Sinai. Among God's imperative commands was one to the effect that they must not associate—let alone marry—with the Canaanite nations. There was an evil strain in these people which was revealed in their history and well understood by the older Bible students. It was proved both by sacred and secular records. Now the current hysteria regarding race has blinded many to obvious facts. Israel was to be the Lord's chosen instrument and must not be contaminated by violent and cruel characteristics. If we turn back the pages of biblical history, there is clear evidence that the destined leaders of the Kingdom nation were subjected to satanic attacks upon their virtue by foreign women, usually of the Canaanite race. Esau married Hittite women and was disinherited by God, in His foreknowledge, even before Esau was born.[4] Now the children of Judah were being dealt with according to their character, like the patriarchs before them. We read very little concerning the clan of Judah's son Shelah, but the little that we know is illuminating. The last reference to them occurs in the genealogies of *Chronicles*, where we read that the descendants of Mareshah, son of Shelah, were "the families of the house of them that wrought fine linen, of the house of Ashbea." The combination of fine linen weaving and the name of Shelah points irresistibly to Ireland. This is no coincidence, for the methods used in Ireland, until the recent introduction of machinery, were exactly the same as those in use in ancient Egypt throughout the whole process of linen weaving. The strange disappearance of the Shelah family from the Bible story and the appearance of the linen weavers in Ireland are facts which dovetail together.

The journey from Egypt to Ireland was by no means unknown,

---

[4] *Genesis* 25:23; 26:34,35

for trade with the ports beyond "the Pillars of Hercules" was common during the Bronze and Iron Ages. It is probable that Shelah would be unpopular with the other tribes of Israel, for wherever the Canaanite is there are hot tempers. So we find that his settlement in Ireland draws others of a like kind, as the centuries pass, many coming from Spain where a similar mingled population was to be found after the dispersion of Canaanites in the time of Alexander the Great. This is by no means the whole story in relation to Ireland, but it does show the introduction of a disruptive element. Later migrations of true Judah people were to follow.

On the Trail of Zarah

Parts of the clan of Zarah undoubtedly came to Spain and Ireland (*vide* names such as Zaragossa, incorporating the family name) and the migrations from Greece brought royal families of that clan. The story of the birth of the twins contains the account of the tying of a scarlet thread on the hand of Zarah.[5] This was thought to be sufficiently important to be placed on record and might well be commemorated in the family emblems, for the question of which of the twins was born first would be a matter of debate in the family. A pamphlet published by the Belfast Museum, dealing with the Red Hand of Ulster, shows this device to be of unknown antiquity and always associated with the Scots of Ulster. Like the linen weaving of Shelah, it is surely more than mere coincidence.

---

[5] *Genesis* 38:28,29

The Twins in Partnership

Nothing happens by chance in Israel's story and the smallest incidents should be noted. The uncertainty as to which of the twins was born first seems to suggest that their inheritance was to be a partnership in which the one actually born first was to be the leader, while the other followed very closely and shared the birthright responsibility which, in this case, was the throne. Although we would not say there was no part of Shelah and Zarah left with the other tribes, it seems certain that, from the Exodus onward, the biblical story of Judah is concerned particularly with the family of Pharez and it is from this house that the family of Jesse and his son David was drawn. This means that Pharez provided the Royal House in Israel, thus fulfilling the promise of the Sceptre given to Judah. It would be unwise to assume that the story of Judah's Sceptre was confined only to the branch of the family that remained in Palestine and this is where the importance of Zarah comes in. There was a westward migration of Hebrews as early as the time of Abraham. They were the circle-building race who has left stone circles all along their route. Then there were portions of Israel that left Egypt before the Exodus. There were the *Danaan,* said by the Greek histories to have crossed from Egypt to Greece. They formed the bulk of the population of Greece before the arrival of the Dorians, who followed overland from Asia.

Many of the *Danaan* migrated later into Ireland and brought with them their own royal family. All Greek history is bound up with mythology, which usually consists of the worship of former heroes, but it is from these heroes that the great families have sprung. The princely families ruling over the city states of Greece kept their genealogies and their right to rulership was acknowledged. Not only the *Danaan* people, but the princely houses ruling over them, point back to Egypt as their place of origin.

The chronology of Archaic Greece is vague. We can only calculate it in generations, but the time of the simultaneous foundation of these Greek dynasties approximates to the period of Calcol and Darda (or Dara), the sons of Zarah. The Rev. William Milner regarded Calcol as the same person as Cecrops, the first King of Athens. This is not just imagination, for it fits into this general picture of the Divine plan for Judah's rulership. The information which we obtain from the Greek classics tells us that Cecrops came from Egypt with his brothers. They were princes, a fact which would certainly apply to the Sceptre tribe. Their number seems vague and we can discount the legend of "fifty brothers," though there could have been fifty in the ship that brought them.

The Greek Dynasties

Cecrops became the first king and founder of Athens. The inhabitants of the country were wild and without discipline. We read that Cecrops set to work organising them, gave them their laws—a significant point this — and generally brought order out of the chaos. He was behaving exactly as a child of Judah might be expected to behave, if he took the Divinely given birthright of rulership seriously.[6]

Nelson's Encyclopaedia describes his work in these words, "To him are attributed the institution of marriage, the abolition of human sacrifice, and the establishment of a purer worship." The fact that Cecrops divided the people into twelve communities suggests either that he followed the arrangements prevailing in twelve-tribed Israel, or that a folk-memory of Israel may have been introduced here. One fact seems certain, that Cecrops took the leadership in appointing the cities which were to be the focal centres of these sections of the nation and appointed his brothers to rule in them. There is no suggestion of

---

[6] *Pausanius* 9:33

oppression in the methods used—quite the contrary—and these earliest kings of Attic Greece are remembered with honour.

The Trojan Kings

At roughly the same period, so far as the chronology can be assessed, the city of Troy, already ancient as we see from archaeology, was visited by Darda. This looks like a concerted effort on the part of the sons of Judah to bring order into the lives of the migrating Hebrews. We can be as certain that Darda was Dar-danos of Troy, as we can be certain of any event in the second millennium before Christ. There was a continual movement out of Asia into Asia Minor, where Troy and its environs became more and more important. The genealogy of Priam, the king who reigned in Troy at the time of the Trojan War, goes back to Dardanos, which is the Greek form of "Darda." Josephus, in dealing with the story of Calcol and Darda, gives Darda's name as "Dardanos," showing that Darda and Dardanos were regarded as one during the first century AD.

The Viking Rulers

As the westward migration proceeded, these royal families of the house of Zarah came with them. It was not yet time for the Royal House of David to be dispersed from Jerusalem. It was to reign, first over Israel, then over the Judah kingdom in Palestine. Meanwhile, the Zarah kings were able to exercise rule of a kind far more wise than was seen in the pagan world. The likenesses between Greeks and Norsemen are seldom observed, yet they are many and particularly with regard to royalty and law. When the Romans required laws, they went to the Greeks for them, because the laws of the Greeks were renowned for their wisdom. Athena, the patroness of Athens and goddess of wisdom, is believed to be the deified wife of Cecrops. Little remains of the actual wording of Archaic Greek laws, but we can see that they were respected, though many, like the Romans, altered them beyond recognition. When the Norsemen began their great migration to the west and north, they were governed by their king Odin. He also was deified, but there is no doubt as to his actual existence, as we can see from the Norse Sagas, in which all the Scandinavian royal families are traced back to the sons of Odin. Many tales are told of their benign rule. Of Skiold, the first King of Denmark, and one of Odin's sons, we are told that the land was so peaceful under his reign that a man might leave a bag of gold in the street all night and find it again next morning. In the prologue to *The Prose Edda,* we read that Odin was descended, by eighteen generations, from Thor who was grandson of Priam, King of Troy.

No doubt the laws of Greeks, Trojans and Norsemen had the same origin. Was it in the laws known to the Hebrews before they were codified at Sinai?

The Saxon Rulers

The two sons of Odin, Baeldeg and Wegdeg, went into "Saxland" and married Saxon women. When, in course of time, the Saxons came into Britain, they brought their own king, Cerdic. In the *Anglo-Saxon Chronicle* the genealogy of Cerdic goes back to Odin. Sir George Bellew, Garter King of Arms, tells us that the method of choosing a new king among the Saxons was that the elders met to make their choice from the family of Cerdic. He need not be a son of the previous king, but he must be descended from Odin. King Alfred the Great was chosen in this way and though he was a wise choice, he was not the eldest son of the former king. This method reminds us very much of God's choice of the rulers in Israel.

The Thrones in Britain

When the Zarah kings of the Saxon house of Odin arrived in Britain, what did they find? Already there was a ruling house in Ireland, having come from the east when the *Danaan* migrated from Greece to Britain. Into that ruling family Tea Tephi was married. She had come from Egypt after the fall of Jerusalem to Nebuchadnezzar. In them were united the families of Zarah and Pharez, both royal houses of high renown throughout the then known world. In Wales, the Silurian royal family was reigning. This had preserved its genealogy showing descent from Brutus the Trojan, who came to Britain about 1000 BC. When Joseph of Arimathea came to Britain, his children married into the Silurian house. Joseph is mentioned in several ancient Welsh genealogies and is named in the triad of "Three Saintly Lineages of the Island of Britain."[7] Another branch of the Trojan family ruled in Colchester and yet other branches provided the kings of North Wales and the Picts. So we find these various families coming naturally together, from the houses of Pharez and Zarah, and all intermarrying, so that our present beloved Queen is descended from them all and unites the various ruling branches of Judah in her own royal person. The people of Ulster were, throughout their history, known as Scots. It was a migration from Ulster which took the name to Scotland. The Scots themselves were named after their ancestress Scota who, according to Irish histories, came from Egypt via Spain where she married a Greek prince named Gathelus. There seems no doubt that the Scots were acknowledged as a royal clan.

---

[7] *Trioedd ynys prydain* 81

The Purpose Fulfilled

So we see the purpose of God being fulfilled. All the royal families of Europe, as well as the nations of purely Israel origin, have been drawn from Judah. It is the family Divinely chosen to hold the Sceptre. It is significant that while the nations of mixed race have thrown off the yoke of royal rule, the Israel nations remain faithful to their monarchy. If God Himself appointed monarchy as the next best form of government to His own Theocracy, there must have been wisdom in that choice. Just as Cecrops knew the people of Attica needed leadership, so the same fact seems to apply throughout our history. We know what happened to the Pharez branch of Judah that remained in Jerusalem, for it was never lost. It provided the House of David which, like the Zarah rulers, was a separate entity detached from the nations over which it ruled, it provided the family of our Lord, who is the supreme Heir of David's line; it provided the earliest Christian missionaries who were closely related to Him and it experienced its own particular dispersion westward, mingling in Christian activity with those Israelites who had already travelled to western Europe and Britain. Meanwhile, the nation of the Jews, associating and intermarrying more and more with the Canaanites, became further and further removed from the birthright of Israel, which is the responsibility for building the Kingdom of God on earth. It will be noticed readily enough, that the two leaderships in Israel, represented by Judah and Joseph, come very closely to the form of constitutional monarchy which works so well in the Israel nations: the monarch at the head and the prime minister functioning on behalf of the people, guiding the practical affairs of the nation.